U.S. PRESIDENTS
MYTHS OR FACTS?

MYTHS AND FACTS ABOUT ABRAHAM LINCOLN

EZRA E. KNOPP

PowerKiDS press

Published in 2024 by The Rosen Publishing Group, Inc.
2544 Clinton Street, Buffalo, NY 14224

Editor: Greg Roza
Book Design: Michael Flynn

Photo Credits: Cover Werkat/Shutterstock.com; (series background) Azamatovic/Shutterstock.com; p. 5 https://commons.wikimedia.org/wiki/File:A%26TLincoln.jpg; p. 7 https://commons.wikimedia.org/wiki/File:Abraham_Lincoln.png; pp. 9, 17, 19 (train) Everett Collection/Shutterstock.com; p. 11 https://commons.wikimedia.org/wiki/File:Abraham_Lincoln_by_Nicholas_Shepherd,_1846-crop.jpg; p. 13 Eddie J. Rodriquez/Shutterstock.com; p. 15 https://commons.wikimedia.org/wiki/File:Abraham_Lincoln_O-74_by_A_Gardner,_1863.jpg; p. 19 (assassination) https://commons.wikimedia.org/wiki/File:Lincoln_assassination_slide_c1900_-_Restoration.jpg.

Library of Congress Cataloging-in-Publication Data

Names: Knopp, Ezra E., author.
Title: Myths and facts about Abraham Lincoln / Ezra E. Knopp.
Description: [Buffalo, New York] : PowerKids Press, [2024] | Series: U.S. presidents : myths or facts? | Includes bibliographical references and index.
Identifiers: LCCN 2023026552 (print) | LCCN 2023026553 (ebook) | ISBN 9781499444025 (library binding) | ISBN 9781499444018 (paperback) | ISBN 9781499444032 (ebook)
Subjects: LCSH: Lincoln, Abraham, 1809-1865–Juvenile literature. | Presidents–United States–Biography–Juvenile literature. | United States–Politics and government–1861-1865–Juvenile literature. | United States–History–Errors, inventions, etc.–Juvenile literature.
Classification: LCC E457.905 .K52 2024 (print) | LCC E457.905 (ebook) | DDC 973.7092 [B]–dc23/eng/20230606
LC record available at https://lccn.loc.gov/2023026552
LC ebook record available at https://lccn.loc.gov/2023026553

Manufactured in the United States of America

CPSIA Compliance Information: Batch #CWPK24. For Further Information contact Rosen Publishing at 1-800-237-9932.

CONTENTS

A TOUGH CHILDHOOD

A very common thing people say about President Abraham Lincoln is that he was raised in a log cabin. This is true! He was born February 12, 1809, in a one-room log cabin near Hodgenville, Kentucky.

Some stories say that Lincoln walked at least 5 miles (8 km) to school every day. However, reports differ, and we can't say for sure if it's true. Historians do know that Lincoln didn't spend much time in school. He spent more time doing hard work on his family's farm.

IT'S A FACT!

LINCOLN HIMSELF ESTIMATED, OR GUESSED, THAT HE HAD RECEIVED ABOUT ONE YEAR OF CLASSROOM SCHOOL TRAINING IN TOTAL DURING HIS CHILDHOOD.

IT'S TRUE THAT LINCOLN DIDN'T SPEND MUCH TIME IN SCHOOL. HOWEVER, HE WAS RARELY SEEN WITHOUT A BOOK IN HIS HANDS. HERE, LINCOLN READS TO HIS SON, TAD, IN 1864.

MYTH OR FACT?

LINCOLN NEARLY DROWNED IN A CREEK AS A CHILD.

MYTH

It's fair to say that Lincoln had to work very hard as a child. We know that Lincoln grew up poor. He sometimes went without food, and sometimes without shoes. His baby brother Thomas died in 1812. The baby was just three days old.

One story about Lincoln's childhood gained popularity in the late 1800s. It said that Lincoln fell into a swiftly moving creek and had to be rescued. However, this is likely just a story. There's no **proof** that it's fact.

SOMEONE MAY HAVE MADE UP THE CREEK STORY TO HELP SHOW HOW **DANGEROUS** LINCOLN'S EARLY LIFE WAS. THIS MADE HIM EVEN MORE LIKABLE.

MYTH OR FACT?

LINCOLN WAS A GREAT WRESTLER.

FACT

As a teen, Lincoln grew tall. He became very strong from all the hard work he did. By the time he was 17, Lincoln was 6 foot, 4 inches (1.9 m) tall and weighed 185 pounds (84 kg)!

His large size and strength allowed him to do well in sports. He was particularly good at wrestling. In those days, wrestling was a lot more **violent**. It was more like hand-to-hand combat! In 12 years, Lincoln lost just one out of 200 wrestling matches.

IT'S A FACT!

LINCOLN WAS VERY SKILLED WITH AN AX, AND HE WAS NICKNAMED "THE RAIL-SPLITTER." THIS IS BECAUSE HE SPENT SEVERAL YEARS "SPLITTING RAILS," OR CHOPPING LOGS TO MAKE FENCE POSTS.

IN 1992, LINCOLN WAS INDUCTED INTO THE NATIONAL WRESTLING HALL OF FAME.

NATURAL-BORN LEADER

MYTH OR FACT?

LINCOLN FIRST RAN FOR POLITICAL OFFICE AT THE AGE OF 23.

FACT

In 1831, Lincoln moved to New Salem, Illinois. It was the first time he had been away from his family. He tried several jobs, including those of shopkeeper, postmaster, and **surveyor**. He soon became interested in local politics. In 1832, Lincoln ran for the Illinois state **legislature** but lost.

That same year, Lincoln **volunteered** to join a **militia** to fight in the Black Hawk War (against members of the Sauk, Fox, and Kickapoo Native American groups). He was quickly made a captain. However, Lincoln never saw battle.

LINCOLN RAN FOR ILLINOIS STATE LEGISLATURE AGAIN IN 1834 AND WON!

MYTH OR FACT?

LINCOLN ATTENDED LAW SCHOOL TO BECOME A LAWYER.

MYTH

After the Black Hawk War, Lincoln thought about becoming a blacksmith. However, he soon decided that becoming a lawyer was a better fit for him. He taught himself many topics, including grammar and math. He learned how to become a lawyer by reading and watching court cases.

Lincoln passed the test to become a lawyer in 1836, when he was just 25. The next year, he moved to the state capital of Springfield, Illinois, where he found more work than in the tiny town of New Salem.

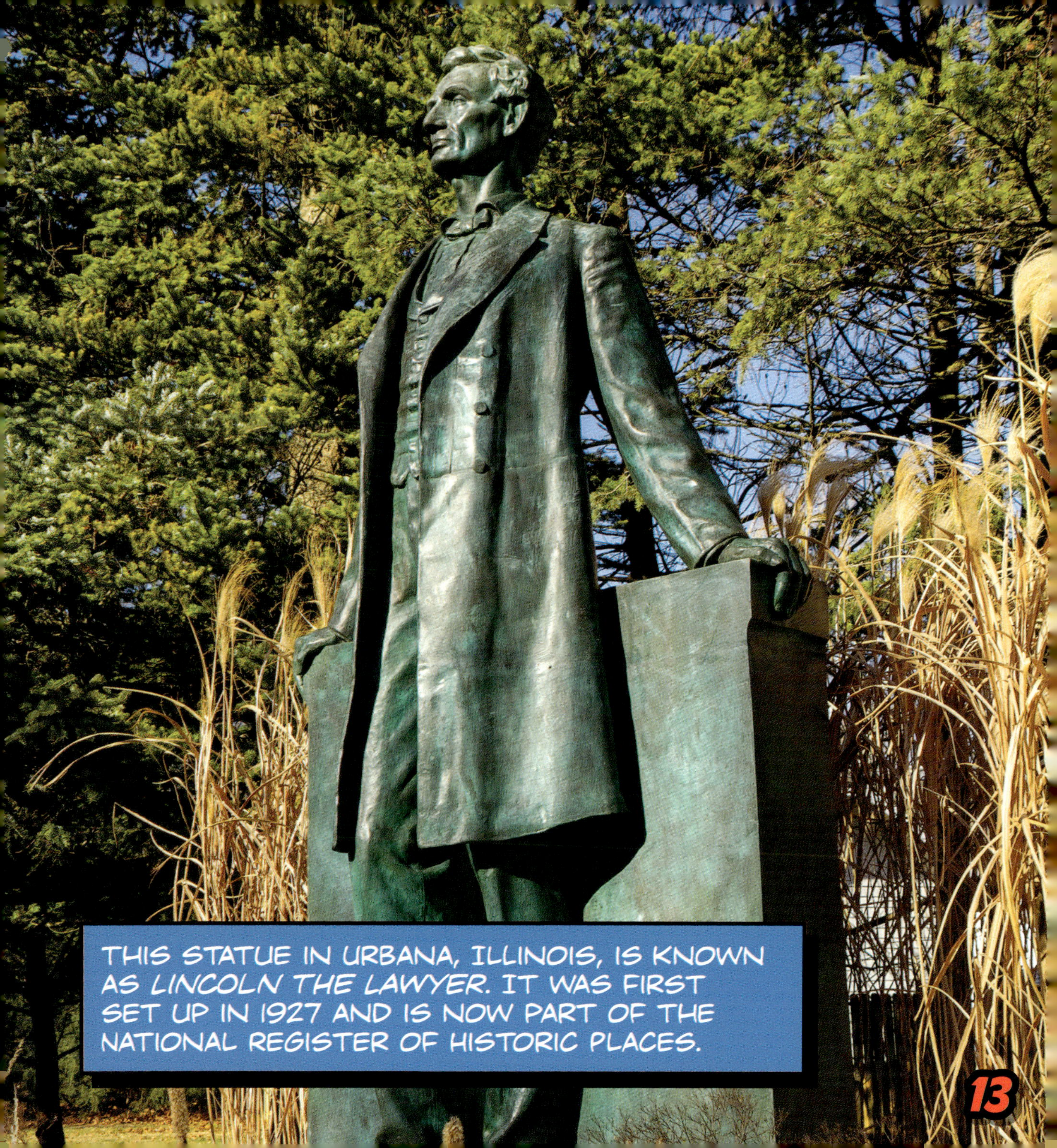

THIS STATUE IN URBANA, ILLINOIS, IS KNOWN AS *LINCOLN THE LAWYER*. IT WAS FIRST SET UP IN 1927 AND IS NOW PART OF THE NATIONAL REGISTER OF HISTORIC PLACES.

MYTH OR FACT?

LINCOLN SUFFERED FROM BAD HEALTH DURING HIS LIFE. AT ONE POINT, HE SUFFERED A BREAKDOWN AND SPENT SIX MONTHS IN BED.

MYTH

One modern belief is that Lincoln suffered from a **disorder** called Marfan syndrome. Signs of this disorder include long arms, legs, and fingers; a tall, thin body; and a sunken chest. However, there's no proof Lincoln had the disorder. It's just a guess.

In 1835, Anne Rutledge, a woman Lincoln loved, died. Today, stories say that Lincoln was so sad he stayed in bed for six months! However, records show that Lincoln continued his surveying and political jobs soon after her death.

IT'S A FACT!

HISTORIANS KNOW THAT LINCOLN SUFFERED FROM THE DISEASES MALARIA AND SMALLPOX DURING HIS YOUNG LIFE.

ALTHOUGH SOME STORIES SAY LINCOLN WAS SICKLY, THAT'S NOT TRUE. LINCOLN WAS VERY FIT!

PRESIDENT LINCOLN

MYTH OR FACT?

LINCOLN WROTE THE GETTYSBURG ADDRESS ON THE BACK OF AN ENVELOPE WHILE ON A TRAIN.

MYTH

The Gettysburg Address is one of the greatest speeches ever written. On November 19, 1863, Lincoln delivered this speech to a crowd of around 15,000 people near the Gettysburg battlefield in Pennsylvania—the location of the deadliest battle of the American Civil War.

Perhaps the greatest myth about the Gettysburg Address is that Lincoln wrote it in a hurry on the back of an envelope while on a moving train. In truth, he wrote several drafts of the speech in the weeks before November 19.

THERE ARE FIVE KNOWN DRAFTS OF THE GETTYSBURG ADDRESS, EACH WRITTEN BY LINCOLN. NONE OF THESE DRAFTS SHOW MESSY HANDWRITING, WHICH YOU MIGHT EXPECT IF LINCOLN WAS WRITING ON A MOVING TRAIN.

MYTH OR FACT?

JOHN WILKES BOOTH, THE MAN WHO ASSASSINATED LINCOLN, ORIGINALLY PLANNED TO KIDNAP HIM INSTEAD.

FACT

On April 14, 1865, Lincoln and his wife, Mary Todd Lincoln, went to a play at Ford's Theatre in Washington, D.C. This was just a few days after the end of the American Civil War. Booth shot Lincoln in the back of the head before fleeing.

Originally, Booth planned to kidnap the president while he traveled. However, this plan failed. He then planned to kidnap Lincoln at the play. However, Booth decided to assassinate Lincoln instead once he learned the South had lost the war.

LINCOLN ASSASSINATION

LINCOLN'S PRESIDENTIAL TRAIN CAR WAS USED AS HIS **FUNERAL** TRAIN. IT TRAVELED FROM WASHINGTON, D.C., TO SPRINGFIELD, ILLINOIS. THE TRAIN STOPPED AT SEVERAL CITIES ALONG THE WAY TO ALLOW U.S. CITIZENS TO PAY THEIR FINAL RESPECTS TO LINCOLN.

LINCOLN'S GHOST?

Lincoln's death was a tragic, or very sad, event in U.S. history. It came at a time when the country was just starting to think about the time after the American Civil War. Many Americans **mourned** the loss of perhaps the country's greatest president.

Today, some people insist Lincoln's ghost still walks the halls of the White House! Even famous guests, including British Prime Minister Winston Churchill, claimed to have seen him. Is Lincoln's ghost a myth or a fact? What do you think?

IT'S A FACT!

THERE'S A ROOM IN THE WHITE HOUSE KNOWN AS THE LINCOLN BEDROOM. THIS ROOM WAS ONCE LINCOLN'S OFFICE.

LINCOLN'S TIMELINE

FEBRUARY 12, 1809	LINCOLN IS BORN NEAR HODGENVILLE, KENTUCKY.
1816	THE LINCOLN FAMILY MOVES TO INDIANA.
1830	THE LINCOLN FAMILY MOVES TO ILLINOIS.
1832	LINCOLN RUNS FOR THE ILLINOIS STATE LEGISLATURE BUT LOSES. HE JOINS A MILITIA AND BECOMES A CAPTAIN DURING THE BLACK HAWK WAR.
1836	LINCOLN BECOMES A LAWYER.
1842	LINCOLN MARRIES MARY TODD.
1846	LINCOLN IS ELECTED TO THE U.S. HOUSE OF REPRESENTATIVES.
1860	LINCOLN IS ELECTED PRESIDENT OF THE UNITED STATES.
1861–1865	THE AMERICAN CIVIL WAR TAKES PLACE.
1864	LINCOLN IS REELECTED.
APRIL 14, 1865	LINCOLN IS SHOT BY JOHN WILKES BOOTH AND DIES A DAY LATER.

GLOSSARY

assassinate: To kill someone, especially a public figure.

dangerous: Not safe.

disorder: A medical condition of the mind or body.

funeral: Having to do with the ceremonies held for a dead person.

legislature: A law-making body.

militia: A group of people who aren't an official part of the armed forces of a country but who are trained like soldiers.

mourn: To show or feel sadness, usually after someone has died.

proof: An act or process of showing or finding out that something is true.

surveyor: A worker whose job is to measure land areas.

violent: Done by using physical force in a way meant to cause harm to someone.

volunteer: To do something to help because you want to do it.

FOR MORE INFORMATION

BOOKS

Harrison, Wag. *The Presidents Did What?* Richmond, VA: Belle Isle Books, 2021.

London, Martha. *Abraham Lincoln*. Los Angeles, CA: North Star Books, 2023.

Shulman, Mark. *Abraham Lincoln: Defender of the Union!* San Diego, CA: Portable Press, 2019.

WEBSITES

Abraham Lincoln
kids.nationalgeographic.com/history/article/abraham-lincoln
Learn more facts about the 16th president at this website.

Biography: President Abraham Lincoln
www.ducksters.com/biography/uspresidents/abrahamlincoln.php
This detailed website has more information about Lincoln, including photographs and links to activities and further information.

Publisher's note to educators and parents: Our editors have carefully reviewed these websites to ensure that they are suitable for students. Many websites change frequently, however, and we cannot guarantee that a site's future contents will continue to meet our high standards of quality and educational value. Be advised that students should be closely supervised whenever they access the internet.

INDEX